T0353786

Sunflower Days

Reflections from
an ordinary mama
on the early years
of motherhood

Written by: Alicia Easton
Illustrated by: Vicki Petrosky

Dedication

For Angelina, Mercedes and Asher, the gifts I don't deserve,

their Daddy for his endless love,

and Jesus Christ, to whom I owe it all.

WestBow Press books may be ordered through booksellers or by contacting:

WestBow Press
A Division of Thomas Nelson & Zondervan
1663 Liberty Drive
Bloomington, IN 47403
www.westbowpress.com
844-714-3454

Interior Image Credit: Vicki Petrosky

Scripture quotations marked (NIV) are taken from the Holy Bible, NEW INTERNATIONAL VERSION®, NIV® Copyright © 1973, 1978, 1984, 2011 by Biblica, Inc.® Used by permission. All rights reserved worldwide.

ISBN: 979-8-3850-2997-6 (sc)
ISBN: 979-8-3850-2998-3 (e)

Library of Congress Control Number: 2024915140

Print information available on the last page.

WestBow Press rev. date: 8/21/2024

WESTBOW
PRESS®
A DIVISION OF THOMAS NELSON
& ZONDERVAN

Contents

Preface

Part 1:

Part 2:

Part 3:

Preface

"These are the best days of your life," he said to me.

I smiled politely at the gently-aging gentleman while simultaneously blinking in utter disbelief. Don't get me wrong, being a mother was an absolute dream come true for me but, having three kids three years and under, had left me feeling a bit worse for wear. I knew there was no way this man could have overlooked my groggy eyes cradled with those too-familiar dark circles; I also knew he had seen and heard the little people next to me with their mismatched outfits and silly sounds. The fatigue from early mornings bookended by nights of broken rest had made me unrecognisable to my former self.

The uncertainty on my face would've been obvious as I contemplated if I could accept his words as truth. Uncertain if I could be everything my children needed me to be, uncertain if I was capable of living up to the mothers before me, uncertain if I had it in me to bear this weighty and profound responsibility that is motherhood. Nonetheless, he smiled back at me, genuinely and knowingly, as if he was privy to a glorious secret I had yet to unearth.

As I've trekked further along the unpredictable path of motherhood I've come to see the profoundness of those eight words.

Before there were little feet bringing pitter pattering sounds to my ears, before there were faces to wipe, before my life was no longer just my own, there was a joy that I had yet to discover. And now I *had* found it in the most humbling of places. Joy that had nothing to do with achievements or letters added after my name but rather everything to do with love.

Becoming a mother has pierced my soul in a remarkably deep way that I'm still coming to understand; a way that has impacted and changed me more than I'll ever be able to fully grasp. Furthermore, it has opened my heart to a love that I didn't know was possible.

The pages of this book are devoted to that joy, that process, the fear, the awe, the beauty, the best days of my life. Narrative, prose, poetry, haphazard thoughts on a page. Here you will find a raw glimpse of Motherhood, in all its forms.

These words were collected on napkins, typed madly into my iPhone or scribbled on random colouring sheets in the midst of moments I didn't want to forget. Some were inspired by other mamas, some authored while cuddling my babies or scrubbing dirty floors and others pieced together on my commute home from work.

My prayer is that you may find words here that resonate with you in your season of motherhood. To know that you are not alone in your celebrations in as much as your challenges and heartache. And to collectively acknowledge the incredible gift it is to be called 'Mama'.

Part 1:

Seedlings

The little sunflowers emerge from the ground reaching upward into the big, wild world; tiny leaves begin to grow.

One: Anthems

An accolade of motherhood

If you're looking for me these days you'll find me here, wrapped up by little arms and captivated by baby blues. Over time, the shades that have made up the backdrop of my world have changed, but I'm still here, camouflaged by stamps and stickers and obnoxiously purple paint.

I've forfeited the more glamorous life for a different kind of happiness. One that's busy and messy but unequivocally magical in its own way.

At first you might not see it, the beauty, but lean in, look closer.

Buried under the piles of books and dress-ups, around sticky placemats with half-eaten grilled cheese sandwiches there's evidence of a simple satisfaction that can't be measured and a contagious, almost palpable kind of joy.

Beneath the steady stream of cries and squeals and boisterous bangs, the seemingly endless symphony of sounds, there's a whisper of wonder, faint enough to overlook if your heart isn't tuned to hear.

It's enveloped me for better or for worse, for cleaner or dirtier, for calm or for the chaos. I wake up each day lost in it, but also found, knowing my purpose has been composed from above.

It's so easy to get caught up in this anthem called motherhood. Maybe you are too. It's an expression of a higher love, a picture of sacrifice. It entrenches deep in your heart and encapsulates your very existence.

I'm partial to its lyrics even if I don't always portray them with perfect articulation. They speak of spontaneous pillow forts, whimsical wildflower quests, somersaults in the front yard, silly bathtime songs and giggles over cups of milk that are more often spilt than not.

They speak of other, deeper things too; tiny victories, hidden struggles, the thick and the thin.

We all sing this anthem differently in different seasons. Sometimes slowly with appreciation for each moment, melodies overflowing with grace and gratitude. Other times quickly, wanting to just get through the more challenging verses, simply hoping we finish those days in one piece. And then there are those times when we laboriously give a half-hearted harmony, grappling with the tension between the notes, weighed down by moments that are unchartered and feel unbearable, beating with a longing for an easier, familiar chorus.

No matter whether you're singing through the last bridge or just waiting for the first verse to start, the song you sing will be powerful and original; the journey you're on is worth celebrating. Sing your anthem with pride, knowing it was written only for you.

Those who know what they're made for radiate
a light that beams the brightest of all.

Two: Constellations

A late-night reflection

It's been three hundred and five hours since you came into the world and already time is slipping away through my fingers too quickly. I try to grab onto it and hold it ransom as I bargain for more but it escapes me, elusively, bringing greater weight and value to each moment we have together.

So between you and me I'll treasure it all.

Those long hours when the rest of the world is dreaming; when our eyelids are heavy I'll fight to stay awake a little longer, not wanting to miss a thing, never wanting to forget you were this small.

Between you and me
we know names of the constellations showing off at midnight and
the call of the first bird as it awakens the dawn.

You know the beat of my heart as I hold you close and I know the rhythm of your breaths, like the steady sound of little waves meeting the shore, each one a cadence of its own, comforting and sweet.

Between you and me
we have an unspoken understanding: I'm here for you always and always will be.

Between you and me
we have lullabies of our own, made with words of hope, joy, anticipation, and love
to carry us both through the days ahead. I wonder where adventure will take you,
of the plans our Creator has for you and about who you will become.

Between you and me
I know you're going to change to change the world because you're already changing mine.

Three: Milestones

Your first step took us all by surprise. Like snow on Thanksgiving, we knew it was possible, but we weren't ready. It was the warm-up before the big game, the preview before the feature film. You took your stance on the edge of the world and let us glimpse what you're capable of.

Your second step came along and this time we were ready. You had a captive audience gawking at your every move. Those clunky, wobbly steps that required every ounce of strength you could muster until gravity stole the show; we knew you were on the brink of something spectacular.

Then your third step came...

And my past and future tenses all collided in a present progressive form. All at once the time that's slipped through my fingers and the dreams I have for what's ahead merge together before my very eyes,

I'm holding you for the first time in the busy hospital room, noises coming from every direction but finding an oasis in the chaos as the warmth of your tiny, soft cheek presses against mine and drowns everything else out.

I'm hearing you first babble my name. Sounds forming to be sweeter than honey and I'm lost in wonder as you look up to me with that sweet, two-toothed grin and your unjustly long eyelashes.

I'm waving goodbye as I drop you off for your first day of school, mustering up all the strength I can find, pretending to be brave as I let you go.

I'm shamelessly cheering you on in the stands during your first footy game, win or lose, wanting everyone to know you belong to me.

I'm watching with tears in my eyes as you stand in front of a girl and promise to be her future, knowing there's no possible way I could be prouder of the man you've become.

My heart races with excitement for you on the day you took your first step just as it always has and always will with your every forward move.

The little steps and the gigantic ones alike, the clumsy steps and the calculated, the uncertain steps and those made with confidence, the reluctant steps and the brave.

This mama's heart is forever tied to your story.

Three steps and the world as we know it is about to change.

Four: Take My Hand

A poem about heart cries

Take my hand
It's all I want
Not your long-winded words of reprimand
Squeeze it so I know you're there
And the tears will stop soon.

Take my hand
When the thunder cracks and the floodwaters rise
When the blustery wind threatens to blow us from our place
The steadiness of you next to me
Is all that I need.

Take my hand
When I'm uncertain
Show me the monsters aren't there
Check under my bed and in the dark corners
Bring light to my shadows.

Take my hand
When I can't explain the way I feel
When my world doesn't make sense
And none of the puzzle pieces fit in
Be my safe hiding place.

Please take my hand
Across the rocks
The bumpy, uneven, muddy trail
Where roots can trip and the terrain is steep
Even though I should do it on my own
Be the one who helps me.

Just take my hand
Be the one who is constant
Bring your calm voice and stability into my world
Envelope me with the comfort of your presence
For knowing you're there is enough.

Take my hand, mama.

Day after day she held his hand so forever
and always he held her in his heart.

Five: Hard Days

Recollections from the trenches

Last night I had been awake feeding my sweet, squishy baby boy and had gotten him back to dreamland when our one-and-a-half-year-old woke up and refused to be settled by anyone who didn't sound and smell like me. After weeks of ups and downs with our girls adjusting to life with a new baby, on top of long nights dealing with sickness and teething, all I was asking for was one night of relative peace. I stayed in bed for as a long as I could hold out, listening to her cries over the monitor as my husband tried his hardest to comfort her. But to no avail, her little yet fierce sobs tugged at my heart forcing me to drag my exhausted body out of bed against its will. I went in and held her. Not sure what she wanted, not sure what was wrong. Very sure she woke up half the neighbourhood. Was it teething? Was she getting sick again? Did she not have enough dinner? Did she not get enough attention during the day? Was she just being a toddler? Nothing was appeasing her so I started crying with her. I cried because I didn't know what else to do, because I knew I didn't have all the answers. I cried because some days are just plain hard.

I hoped deep down that my tears were communicating to her what my words couldn't, "Baby girl, I love you. I'm here for you. I'm trying my best, I really am. Most days I have no idea what I'm doing but I do know, without a doubt, that I love you immensely and I want that to be enough." When she realised I was crying too, she calmed down for a moment, reached up and put her chubby little hands on my cheeks. A wave of relief came over us both as if we had reached the eye of a storm, a momentary respite from the raging winds of frustration and relentless downpour of emotion as I hoped she understood that my heart was *for* her completely.

It's on the hard days that I feel this need to be everything as a mum. I want to wake up early each day and have a beautiful homemade breakfast waiting for them at the table. I want to respond to every cry and complaint with a calm and patient spirit. I want my family to only see my grace-filled side topped with energy, cheeriness and positivity.

Instead, the reality these days is that I'm typically rolling out of bed in the last few minutes before my husband heads to work, trying to steal as many winks of sleep as possible. It's a lucky day for them if I get into the shower and out of my exercise clothes before noon let alone prepare any sort of breakfast besides yours-truly Cheerios. And I know there are many times my discipline technique is not up to 'Mary Poppins-standards'.

Some days I give my kids chocolate just so they'll stop being whiny. I'll let them watch way more than the recommended amount of daily screen time. I've also found myself swaddling my son to sleep in my sweatshirt because I spent the kids' naptime with Netflix instead of with the laundry room. And I may or may not even find myself online from time to time researching where to find a live-in housekeeper.

But as I sit with mamas older and wiser than me and pour out my heart and frustrations, what I find is that what actually is *most important* is that our kids, our families, the people in our lives see and feel our hearts for them. Some days we will be organised and on top of things and some days we won't be. We are only human after all. God gives us new grace every morning if we accept it, and He gives us each other if we chose to open up and be real.

Some days are hard.

Some days are messy.

Some days nothing happens on time and nothing gets done.

The answer is found in realising and accepting that these days, both the good and bad are inevitable. So from one sleep deprived mama to another be encouraged that in your hard days, no matter what you may feel, you're not alone. We all have struggles and triumphs. We all have strengths and weaknesses. There is much beauty in vulnerability, as hard as it can be, but you never know who will be uplifted when you share your story.

Some days will be hard and it's okay.

The beauty of our days is found where we choose to see it.

Six: The Different Kind of Days

Pandemic reflections

"What kind of day is it mommy? Is it the different kind?"

I look outside. The sun shines brightly into my squinty eyes as I feel its warm rays bypass the window glass and spread across my cheeks. The blue backdrop behind is nothing short of extravagant and it beckons us, but my stomach begins to sink as I acknowledge that although most days like this would typically be spent at the beach or with friends at a café or scouting out the perfect perch for a picnic, now I must reply,

"Yea, honey, it's the different kind."

And from the repertoire of words that I never imagined I would need but have been drawing upon almost daily, I try to find some that will soothe their perplexed and wondering hearts....

"Today we may have to stay at home, so others can stay well, like when we hide out with Barbie and Elsa in our polka-dotted tepee until the rambunctious tickling dinosaur turns back to regular Daddy.

"Today may be lonely, you may miss your friends more that your little self can put into words and tears may sneak out and slide down your cheeks, but don't you fret, because even princesses cry and Spider-Man himself sometimes feels sad.

"Today our most wonderful plans may have to change, and so will we. We will learn to adapt, taking on new colours like a clever stick bug who blends into a branch or an arctic fox who uses the cold, white snow to keep himself safe.

"Today we may have to be brave even when our insides knot up and nothing feels the same, but we can smile anyway, belt out our favourite songs loud enough for the neighbours to hear and dance in our pyjamas all the way to dinnertime if we want to.

"Today we might not know what's coming next. So we'll have to focus on now, setting records for the highest trampoline jumps and tallest towers and biggest bubble mountains in the bath; getting lost in our Crayola creations and messy muffin making until we find another day has already passed and all we are left with is thankfulness.

"Today we may need to give to other people in ways we haven't before, to change how we live life and let go of much, but in all that releasing we can rediscover the extent to which God takes perfect care of us.

"Today may feel strange, it may be hard and different but...

"Every day we can hold hands and you can squeeze tighter when it all gets to be too much.

"Every day we can watch butterflies make their graceful landings on that little stone wall in our front yard, admiring their freedom, and marvel at the simplest of things like your brother's hectic hair after naptime and the gloriousness of chocolate chip pancakes for breakfast.

"Every day we can stretch out on the grass and trace the outlines of the clouds with our fingers making them come alive, lighting up our imaginations with stories and memories and dreams for other days, then when daylight is replaced with darkness we can be swept away together into the galaxies of the night sky.

"Every day we can pray. For what we're missing, for what we long for, for those out of our reach; for hope to be tangible and peace to take over so that we'll come out the other side stronger and more filled with love."

"Someday life will go back to normal, Mommy."

And that I don't know. So I just smile and cuddle her up as tightly as I can.

In a small way we've now joined in with the hymn of mothers and fathers from so many ages. Those who've learned to sing lullabies at decibels loud enough to drown out the boisterous sounds of angry men at war. Who've perfected the art of finding just enough- for their little ones in places of dust and depravity and famine. Who've gone to great extents to build good lives for the sake of their children amidst confusion and chaos.

I hope that we echo their songs well by our responses to our children today. That our little ones look back on this time and see, as challenging as it was, how it transformed our families, drew us closer together, stripped back the excess and rejuvenated our sense of purpose.

At the end of the day, I want them to know that different days can be filled with much goodness too.

Because some days, a mama needs a field full of flowers.

Seven: I Knew You Already

An exhale of loss

They said it was too early to notice, too early to count
But I knew you already
I counted you
From the very moment I knew you existed
You were part of me, and you'll never not be.

The injustice of never counting your fingers
The loss of never kissing your cheeks
The unfairness of not watching you blink that first light into your eyes
It's all lodged in my heart with a blurred image of you
One that I've tried to bring into focus amidst questions unanswered and longings denied.

Because I imagine your laugh and the sound of your voice
I imagine that you would've had your daddy's eyes and your sister's smile
I see the spot at the table that you would've filled
And I know I would have loved you fiercely
Yet I love you still, I always will.

The reality of the world I walk through sits blatantly juxtaposed against the reality of the world had you
been by my side
If you had been here holding my hand
But you were too good for this place with its shadows that block the sun
And now you belong to the kingdom of light
And I miss you my sweet one, forever I will.

Eight: **Hold On**

A vocalisation of hope

Hope.

Hold onto it in the early mornings

Hold onto it late into the night.

Let it guide your laboured footsteps

Let it push you forward in your weariness.

Embrace it in moments of plenty

And may it embrace you when you're lacking much.

Let it revive you in dry deserts

Let it refresh you near bountiful springs.

As you plant and sew and harvest

As you navigate snot, sweat and tears

Hope.

May it sustain you

In seasons of wanting.

May it support you

Like a dear friend.

Hope in what is eternal.

Hope when there is nothing else left to do.

Hope for that which you cannot yet see.

"But the eyes of the Lord are on those who fear him, on those whose hope is in his unfailing love." Psalm 33:18 NIV

Nine: Motherhood

An ode of surrender

Motherhood, it's a place for us to find God. For us who long for it to be, for us whose hearts ache for what's been lost. For us who have known our mothers and us from whom that knowledge has been taken away- He meets us there.

And for us who have the undeserved privilege of bearing the name 'mama,' motherhood brings us to a place where dependency on our human strength must end and the all-sufficiency of Christ must take over.

Motherhood invites us to His table of restoration, where we accept the cup He places in our hands savouring the fact that He'll never leave us to journey alone. Where we can taste and see that the Lord is good in moments of wonder, weakness, beauty and uncertainty alike.

Motherhood reminds us of our desperate need for new mercies every morning often in the form of strong coffee. As we teach and nurture as we discipline and guide, we must daily draw from the richness of all that He bestows.

Motherhood brings us back to the drawing board. Where we're not just erasing crayons from the walls and scrubbing stains from clothes but redefining everything we thought we knew. Where we discover our identity is in Christ alone and His thoughts toward us. Not in what we're able to provide or our qualifications for the job but in that we've been ordained by God *Himself* for a mission stretching far *beyond* ourselves.

It's an opportunity to practise the persistence of prayer, to embody the essence of servanthood and to pour out an endless flow of grace. Where coming to Him on our knees is our only chance of survival- so we come- shirts covered in spaghetti sauce or muddy fingerprint smudges, and here we find our Saviour.

Motherhood shows us we aren't going to have all the answers. For the future of our families, for what could have been done better or what we should do now, but we can submit to the Father who is sweetly omniscient.

It allows us to glimpse the heart of God and the depth of His love as we look into precious little faces expectant for affirmation, protection and direction. And in our desire to give them all those things and more, we dimly mirror the incredible desire of our Heavenly Father for us His children.

It's a mantle through which we're privileged to shape the future, to sew love, hope, wisdom, strength and truth into this world beyond our days.

Ten: From My Kitchen Sink

A celebration of ordinary moments

The cold water runs over my hands as I stand at the kitchen sink, taking an eternity to heat up. But I don't mind, after all, it's Friday night and I have a front row seat to the most beautiful gig in town.

My family.

I watch them as if in a dream, whirling and twirling around me- the girls in their oversized princess dresses omitting gleeful shrills of laughter which echo off our walls filling our home with a radiant, joyous atmosphere. They're chased in circles through the hallway and then back outside again by their daddy who takes the form of tickle monster or cheeky crocodile depending on the nominated make-believe occasion. Little brother is watching too. He gazes at them from the perch of his highchair, fixated on their every move. Over the steady stream of water, I can hear him offering his own canary-like squeals of delight whenever a flash of lacey pink whizzes past him. He seems to know that emitting particularly cute noises and making eye contact with the royalty will cause them to detour and exchange his offerings for slobbery kisses or a mimicked coo.

The magnificent movement is only interrupted temporarily for water breaks or by minor tragedies like stumbles over the corner of the carpet, tiny scratches or squabbles over whose turn it is to hold Mr. Piggy. But just as fast as they happen, they're also forgotten and the colourful merry-go-round resumes.

The water finally starts to feel warm accurately reflecting the state of my soul. As I treasure this scene, I can feel myself holding close every sweet moment with them I've accumulated in the volumes of my heart. All at once, the memories of first glimpsing their faces, those countless endearing words they've uttered, the giggles, the cuddles, the wonder...it all comes rushing back to me.

It's enough to make me forget the painfully long tantrum earlier followed by the nap boycott that went down just hours before. And it's more than enough to remind me how incredibly blessed I am. Being fully present in our world is a lost art, but a secret gift that we as mothers must be resolved to rediscover. Slowing down so not to miss the commonplace but profound goodness around us.

And it appears that this can happen even when washing the dishes.

For such a task as this, by God's grace, I will give my all.

Eleven: Shiny Things

A memoir on comparison

I glanced across the café as I waited in line, holding my little man in one arm, a bulging nappy bag lopsidedly dangling from the other. The girls danced and dodged around my legs as I strained to stay vertical. While I perused the menu, my gaze stopped in its tracks as I saw a mom with her two children similarly aged to mine. They were sitting perfectly postured in their designer clothes, daintily drinking their milkshakes as if they couldn't fathom any other way to behave and chatting in soft voices that floated back and forth effortlessly across the table akin to unicorn breath.

Her life was so shiny.

I found myself wondering for far too long how this super-hero woman gets her hair to comply to all of her wishes, what supplements she must give her kids to make them so peaceful. In the shine of her life, mine reflected back abruptly in my face… there I was, dishevelled, far less symmetrical, a mere cavewoman in comparison. We had rocked up to the café in our aging Toyota Corolla wagon known *only* for its durability and fumbled out of said vehicle it in a very haphazardly manner. Furthermore, in my desperation to ingest some caffeine, I couldn't guarantee that all shoes were even accounted for. As we sat down at a table, I noticed the remnants of some little person's breakfast decorated the shoulder of my shirt where a face had been buried earlier. Cute. And as if that wasn't enough, the two girls now seemed to be having a contest of who could most accurately be mistaken for a relative of the elephant with the loudest spitting sounds. Before long, this sense of insufficiency took over and I could feel my heart sink. Out of nowhere this feeling that who I am and what I have were suddenly not enough.

Comparison. The joy thief. The contentment killer. The purpose de-railer.

To me she seemed to embody motherhood at its finest. Having practically fallen straight off the page of a magazine, she was the epitome of some subconscious definition I'd concocted for myself that demanded to be attained as a mother.

'Mummy?' I snapped back to reality and looked at the three pairs of blue eyes now sitting with me at the table. They didn't care about the smudge on my shoulder or the way my hair looked. They were unaffected by the means through which we got to the café but were purely excited to be there.

This is where I must check my heart, to make sure it is positioned for an accurate perspective with a posture of gratitude. For the truth is, we weren't meant to look at our lives in the reflection of the shininess of others, but in the goodness of Jesus. He gazes at us with unjudgmental, unconditional, incomparable love.

I don't know who your 'her' is, the shiny one, it could be one but it's likely to be many. This lady in the cafe had no idea of my thoughts towards her just as I had no idea what her actual story was. I hadn't walked in her shoes, as cute as they may have been and, therefore didn't know her struggles, what kept her awake at night, what she sacrificed in the past, the regrets she had or burdens she carried.

Our earthly measures of shiny and dull are subjective and faulty, leaving much to be wanting. We most hold our lives and hearts to a higher standard, in light of the One who matters the most.

"The Lord does not look at the things people look at. People look at the outward appearance, but the Lord looks at the heart." 1 Samuel 16:7 NIV

Twelve: **Baby Book**

A series of flashbacks

Newborn

Tiny breaths bringing delicate beginnings

The most delightful and piercing of sounds

First giggles and those bottom two teeth

Learning to make smiles, point fingers and wiggle toes

Leaving us captivated through tired, bleary eyes.

One

Moving everything out of reach

Eyes wide-open taking the world in

Explorations from dawn to nightfall

Naming and chewing the world around you

Finding ourselves joyfully exhausted.

Two

Combining words and movements

Wobbles turning into more confident steps

Discovering exactly what your body can do

Playing the days away under bright, sunny skies

Living life on our toes.

Three

Letting the world know who you are and what you want

Telling your versions of stories that couldn't get any sweeter

Dancing, jumping, throwing, make-believing

Pushing the boundaries and learning your limits

Constantly melting our hearts.

Four

Asking questions endlessly

Taking new risks and discovering your strengths

Starting to understand your feelings and the power in they hold

Making your own plans

Stepping back and letting you soar.

Her voice was the one that their hearts were most tuned to hear.

Thirteen: **Enough**

Before the sun ascends silently upon the horizon, before sleepy little eyes blink in the first ray of light, she forces herself to wake.

Her arms are weary and so is her heart but as her feet hit the cold floor, she commits to what must be done for the day.

Her hands toil to make beauty out of little, crafting the simplest of pleasures in the most unexpected places to bring forth squeals of delight from her little ones.

She sacrifices in ways she never thought she would have to, an instinctive response to an unspoken vow. As a liturgy she gives away her time, her strength, her sleep, her soul all in the name of love.

Her sweat and tears are shed in the making. Giving when she has nothing else to give. Pushing forward with every ounce of power in her being. Somehow managing to feed mouths, wipe tears, give hugs and leave time to listen.

She labours in ways that no one else will see. Familiar with a daily grind that has worn her down but understanding it to be the price that comes from bearing the name.

She races to keep up but feels like she's falling short, with glamourous tales of motherhood reflected by perfectly staged selfies flashing in her peripheral, she takes a breath and focuses on putting one foot in front of the other, bracing for all that must be done and redone tomorrow.

Writing another chapter in an age-old story of struggle and the fiercest of loves she leaves her mark. She wears her jewels in the number of kisses planted on her face and the plethora of scribbly drawings that bear her resemblance. She is admired because she says 'yes' every day to the people that matter most and knows when to raise her hand to say she can't do it on her own. And she is renown. Not because of perfection or failure but because every day in the triumphs and defeats she is there, she is called 'mama' and that is enough.

Fourteen: **Tantrum**

An expose on a timeless conundrum

Our eyes lock. We both know what's coming.

I take a deep breath in and brace for impact. You take a deep breath in, and all hell breaks loose.

You've got fire in your belly that billows up to your eyes and out of your ears. You become a lion who's escaped from the zoo and is determined to avoid re-captivity. You're like a ferocious, exotic species of bird demanding to be heard above everything else. And you're as sly as a slithering snake, confounding my tried and trusted methods of mediation, finding sneaky new ways of exerting your will.

You have a resistance and resolve that astounds me. It leaves me stunned and speechless- in crowded check-out lines, silent libraries, hectic playgrounds. Just when I thought life was under control, we welcomed the 'Age of the Tantrum,' one to undoubtably go down in history for our family, and for some unlucky bystanders, as the age that couldn't end fast enough.

But once the dust from your stomping feet has settled, your raging tears have subsided and all is right in your world again, all that matters is that you know this...

Whenever your heart aches and bursts into a million emotions, mine follows suit.

When you shed those tears, they spill out of my eyes just the same.

When you feel frustration take over your body, it spreads to my chest as well.

When you're afraid, my stomach knots up in empathy.

When anger explodes out of your powerful little lungs, my body clenches in response.

It doesn't matter the length of your wails, the decibels of your cries, the sting of your words, as nonsensical or hurtful as they may be, I'll be there. Sitting on the cold tiles in the bread aisle talking you down. I'll be there. Whispering gently in your ear as your cries rattle the shelves of the unsuspecting books and the glasses of the poor little librarian during story time. I'll be there. On the playground with wood chips clogging up my shoes, dodging through the other children just to get to you. Go ahead run through the fire, sweet one, run. And I'll chase you right through it.

In every tantrum, I'll search for the secret to disarm your heart. I'll trudge through the murky jungles of dysregulation, making a path amidst the myriad of emotions blocking the way. I'll untangle you from those vines, resist as you may, and pull you back to me. Be assured, no matter the obstacles, I *will* find a way to get through, to be there for you. That's what we mamas do.

Come what may, come what may little one. Your fight may be fierce, but my love for you is fiercer and always will be.

Fifteen: Hospital Bed

Reflections on chronic illness

We've been here too many times before. Me sitting next to you in this rubbery, brown, leather-like chair. The nurses coming in and out, out and in, shift changes happening in an endless cycle. Vitals are gathered more times than I can count, and I'm confident I could take them myself by now.

Time seems warped and surreal. The sterile smell that surrounds us, both sickens and comforts me. The sudden swoosh of the curtains drawn around your bed startles me every time and makes me confront the harsh reality of just exactly where we are. I've memorised the patterns of the tiles on the ceiling while I've held you against my chest. I've counted your breaths alongside your heartbeats as the machine attached to you beeps with a steady rhythm. The sound that determines how long we will have to stay in this place, the sound that reminds me of your fate.

I pray a weary but sincere prayer that your body can fight this fight again, that you can withstand all that is thrown against you. Because when we arrive in this place, I've done everything I could possibly do, but it wasn't enough. You're in a state of complete vulnerability and I must entrust you to the care of the people most qualified. Your body must rally and I'm entirely helpless in all the ways that seem to matter.

But what I know how to do is to hold your hand and stroke the tears off your face when the needles come. And I press my forehead against yours when the mask is put over your mouth once more and we breathe together. And sing you your favourite songs over and over again and do all the silly faces to bring you some sunshine. And I won't sleep, so you can, while I hold you in the awkward position that you're most comfortable in.

I can't deny that seeing you in this constant state of distress has worn me down. It's a battle we didn't ask for and, no matter how many times it happens, one I never feel prepared to handle. Nonetheless, just when I thought we couldn't do it again, you come out fighting. Against the odds, you come out stronger and more resilient. With each trial the capacity of my heart increases as *you* teach *me* to be brave. And though each time I hope we never have to do it again, I know that we can if we must.

Because though you are small, you are the mightiest of heroes.

Sometimes we need the chill of the frost and the scorch of the sun to allow true resilience and unshakable strength to emerge.

Sixteen: **Without You, Without Me**

A voicing of impossible words

I stare at the blank paper for what seems like eternity.

Trying to scribe words that I never want to become our reality.

Me without you, you without me.

Six words that should never be.

I look at them resting on the page where they don't belong and fight the tears back, feeling the sting. Words I wish weren't possible to combine.

Words that simply don't fit grammatically, semantically or pragmatically.

Words that are themselves darkness and extract all light.

Words I can't actually comprehend.

The world isn't fair, this much I know. I've seen heartbreak come storming in where it didn't belong, ravaging families with its merciless gales; the fragility of life exploding abruptly in front of my very eyes, reminding me that time is not ours to keep. We don't get to decide when we come or when we go; there is unbearably so much outside of our control in this broken world.

So what can I do? How can I live knowing these words are possible to breathe into existence while simultaneously taking it all away.

All I can do is surrender.

Every day I will trust in the Giver and Taker of life.

I will depend on Him who is both the Beginning and the End.

I will live my life on my knees praying for eternity.

And trust that, no matter what happens in this life, one day we will be together forever again.

Seventeen: This Mum

Thoughts on unconditional love

'I love this mum.'

He whispered these words in my ear tonight, wrapping his arms tightly around my neck and immediately I felt life rush into my heart. Today those words weren't bestowed after being given a treat or some extra screen time or after surprising him with an unexpected play date. Instead, as he spoke them tonight, I was acutely aware of how entirely undeserving I was to receive them. He gave these words to me without knowing the power that they held. Showing me a love that wasn't limited or conditional or wavering.

Just love.

He didn't care about the misunderstanding at work that I was re-playing through my head a million times or the jobs around the house I didn't get done. He didn't know the inner-battle I was having with myself about decisions I had yet to make. There was no judgement, there were no pre-requisites or expectations. What I have or didn't have, who I might wish I could be or who I am not were irrelevant. His words weren't contingent on anything I had done but simply acknowledged that I was made for him and he was made for me and that was all that was needed.

His words made me pause and consider how freely I am giving love to those around me, made me think about the times I might withhold love from someone until I feel they deserve it or feel that it has been earned. Thank you, sweet boy, for showing me a love that is limitless, for teaching me about its richness and for helping me to remember that the meaning of life lies completely in love.

Oh, that we would open our eyes to see this love, open our hands to give it freely and open our hearts stay teachable to learn from our children.

She was the one they dreamed of becoming.

Eighteen: **Someday Soon**

A list of sacred memories

Someday you'll be older and so much wiser than me
You'll pack your own lunches and drive yourself to school
You'll call your friends for advice and I'll undoubtably embarrass you in from of them.

So for now, I'll treasure in my heart the little things I don't want to forget:

The pure wilderness of your hair when you first crawl out of bed in the morning
The not-so-subtle sound of the fridge door when you're after a sneaky treat
Drawing pictures of animals on each other's backs as we lay sleepily in your bed
Hearing you sing yourself to sleep
Watching you decide whether you want your toast cut into squares or triangles
Pretending to be surprised by your pranks just to see that look of delight on your face
Letting you do fancy styles in my hair and hiding the tears streaming down
my face as I learn the truth about head and scalp sensitivity
Finding your cheeky selfies all over my camera reel
Seeing you prance around the house in my high heels
The way you grab onto my leg when we meet someone new
Hearing your feet on the hardwood floor as you run to jump into our bed in the mornings
Listening to you rattle off random facts about ants and skyscrapers at dinner.

Knowing they won't last forever makes me treasure them more
And I've written them all on my heart.

Part 2:

Flowering

Green shoots strengthen and climb towards the sky; buds form and gradually open into petals.

Nineteen: **Moments**

A haiku collection

Brand new beginnings
It's taken me by surprise
How much I love you.

Lazy morning light
Pillow forts, crayons and blocks
Dreaming days away.

Reach up for the stars
Just glance my way once or twice
When you become one.

Butterfly kisses
Sweet dandelion wishes
Blown by with the breeze.

Christmas dawn waking
Surprise, wonder and delight
Wrapped in packages.

Saltwater and sand
Between our fingers and toes
Seashells and castles.

Jungle adventures
Under canopies of green
Trekking together.

First puppy cuddles
Pouncing, licking, and chasing
Our mini best friend.

Scraped knees on sidewalks
Fixed with Band-Aids and kisses
But you won't be stopped.

School days abounding
You've found your voice and your song
Up, up and away.

With water and sunshine one can bloom in the most unexpected places.

Twenty: Sticks and Stones

Thoughts on matters of the heart

We went for a jog to the park, just the two of us. I pushed her in the pram and tried to conceal my laborious breathing as I answered the obvious, yet profound questions that the wind blew from her little lips back to my ears. Her blonde hair glowed in the late afternoon sun, her dimpled, rosy cheeks were brighter than ever, the fresh air making her come alive.

We studied the shapes of the clouds and wondered where all the animals were hiding; she made an A for her name out of sticks and told me Chloe at school didn't want to be her best friend anymore.

It was matter of fact, a passing comment, like a breath, she merely exhaled it, but I knew it was coming from a deeper place within her tiny three and three quarters year-old heart.

This was the start of what has been, by far, one of the hardest things for me about parenting. Not the surrendering of my body to the feat of growing little humans, nor the many sleepless nights, not even the epic tantrums. It's this...

Watching my kids react when rejection and disappointment and broken heartedness enter into their little worlds. When the princess isn't just playing hide and seek with the prince, but must now face the scary, green, googly-eyed monster. When they realise that words aren't just for singing songs and reading books but can actually cause pain. When they are left out and excluded or misunderstood. It's my absolute least favourite part of parenting.

How do I reconcile these hurdles for my daughter, for my children? Because, if I'm being honest, I want to chase the monster down myself and send him back to where he came from. I want justice for her and apologies to be made. I think back to my childhood and the times that I faced rejection, the times I was made fun of or pushed aside. Things that I subconsciously hoped my children would be able to somehow escape from. Oh, how I wish I was able to preserve their innocence longer, and they could remain untouchable from the unfairness around them. But in our fallen and broken world, I know that run and hide as I want them to, inevitably challenges will come, and the sooner they can learn to face them with confidence, the better.

Maybe I'm a hopeless cause because the heartbreak we're dealing with here is of very small proportion, a tiny ripple compared to the bigger waves of challenges that could be on the horizon in the days ahead. But for now, *these* hardships form the mountain she is on and there are three things I know I can do:

I'll be there with her. As she climbs the difficult terrain, as she navigates through unknown waters, I'll be her confidant, her cheerleader, her friend.

I'll surround her with others, as much as it's in my power, who love, support and believe in her.

I'll point her to Jesus. For in these heartbreaks, as miniscule as they may seem, therein lies the perfect opportunity to speak to my daughter of the love of Christ, who himself bore the brunt of every heartache we face or pain we could come know. I will teach her to make much of Jesus in all her moments and demonstrate this to her by the way I live and rely on Him. For the resurrection power of Christ applies to her life on the playground just as much as it does to the healing of the sick, the lame and the blind.

So when we are at the park studying the shapes of the clouds and wondering where the animals are hiding; when she makes an A for her name out of sticks and tells me Chloe doesn't want to be her friend... I'll tell her she is loved, she is valued and though the mountain seems steep and impassable, by the grace of God, we will climb it together.

Twenty-One: **The First Day of School**

Reflections on the monumental firsts

It feels like only yesterday when I held you for the first time, your tiny fingers fitting so perfectly inside the palm of my hand.

The kind of love that's instantaneous and all-consuming and made me want to never let go.

From that moment on, I've held ever so tightly to that hand. As you braved your first steps and learned to venture up the stairs; as you dared to leap across stones in creek beds and we jumped together over waves crashing on the shore. Here holding my hand is where you learned the beginnings of bravery and to ask questions about the world. Holding my hand is where you discovered that you could get back up after you fell down.

Our days chasing sunlight and muddy puddles and every kind of adventure have been the sweetest kind of bliss. I'll always want to hold you this close forever, but there's an undeniable undertow that is beckoning you to take on the world without me.

So little by little I've been letting you go.

Knowing it's the only way for you to climb higher

The only way for you to run farther

The only way you can lay hold of those distant dreams made just for you

Knowing there's so much more for you to learn than I can teach you myself.

And today, in a grander gesture than I've managed before, I let go of your hand.

Wearing a school bag that's almost bigger than you, walking into a room of new faces, turning back at me with your determined smile on, I let you go.

They'll know their light is worth sharing with the world when they see you shining yours.

Twenty-Two: **Hairbrush**

Everyday musings

It's just you and me while I'm brushing your hair.

We marvel at life's little mysteries.

I ask you my questions.

You tell me the plans for your day,

And repaint your wild dreams from last night.

While I'm brushing your hair

We unpack the ups and downs of your friendships.

I tease through the knots as gently as I can.

Some are harder to untangle than others,

But with time, we are always able to smooth them out.

While I'm brushing your hair

We comb through the waves of everyday encounters.

The new song you heard yesterday,

Daddy's attempt at another funny joke,

And the hard things like fractions at school and politics in the playground.

While I'm brushing your hair

You tell me exactly the style you want.

Trying my best to tame the cowlicks and bumps,

Pulling any stray hairs back in line,

And we both learn that some things don't turn out as we planned.

While I'm brushing your hair
The world passes us by.
Morning after morning, night after night.
Braids and plats, ponytails and buns,
Shaping life together.

All while I'm brushing your hair.

Twenty-Three: **Forgive Me**

An ode of repentance

Forgive me, my sweet one, this mama's still learning.
I'm sorry for my thoughtless words of frustration
For my patience wearing thin
And for not listening to each of your stories with my full attention
For not being fully present when you've needed me most.

Forgive me
For letting the worries of my world creep into yours
For expecting too much of you
And talking the talk but not walking the walk
For all the times I should've said 'I'm sorry' but my pride got in the way.

Forgive me
For holding too tightly when it's been time to let go
For allowing my fear to hold you back from allowing you to learn yourself
For not giving you space and permission to feel the big feelings
And experience life for yourself amongst both the thrills and hazards of the world outside.

Forgive me
For losing sight of what is most important
And for rushing off to the next thing instead of sitting with you a little longer
For forgetting how briefly you'll be little and how fast you will grow
For you deserve all the time and love in the world
Forgive me, my sweet one, this mama's still learning.

Twenty-Four: **Seasons**

Thoughts on the passing of time

The clock ticks steadily behind me

Your gentle coos coincide with the rhythm

Your bassinet cradles you perfectly

Outside my window, crimson leaves twirl in response to the breeze

I watch them settle pleasantly in place on the ground.

I glance up again and its quarter past the hour

You crawl towards me and nestle in for a cuddle

Your nose scrunches up as you giggle at my silly faces

The winter sun peeks in cheekily through the blinds

I'm struck by the beauty of the barren branches, knowing the splendour of the season coming.

The clock chimes at half past

A mishap puzzle lays between us as we sit cross-legged on the carpet

Your fingers scour to find the piece to make the right fit

The birds are chirping noisily outside, flittering from tree to tree

The faint smell of the blossoming jasmine reaches us.

When I look next, it's quarter to the hour

Your uniform sits abruptly on end of your bed, preparing us all for tomorrow

Your chest rises and falls as I watch you sleep so peacefully

The summer air flows in through the open window

The flora outside is luscious and in full bloom.

The clock strikes twelve again

Your tiny fingers curl around just one of mine

You're wearing the onsie that was your sister's as you're nestled in that same bassinette

The air has turned cool, I tuck the blanket in tighter

Autumn is here once more, seasons proceeding without ceasing.

Little did they know that blossoms with such astounding
brilliance could grow from the tiniest of seeds.

Twenty-Five: Honest Confession

A real mama's rhetoric

Sometimes I let you draw on the walls because you were just loving it so much

And stay up too late because doing bedtime can be plain exhausting.

I let you say 'flamly' for 'family' long after it was developmentally appropriate because it was ridiculously cute.

Sometimes I make brownies and hide them from you and your daddy because chocolate is life,

And let you wear the same clothes two days in a row because laundry is not life.

Sometimes I spy on you playing in your room and talking to your toys because it melts my heart,

And climb into your bed when you're asleep to give you extra cuddles after you've had a tricky day.

Sometimes the tooth fairy is a couple days late because she is just really forgetful,

And I may just do your homework for you because sometimes other things are simply more important.

Sometimes we have chicken nuggets for both dinner and lunch just because we wanted to,

And have popsicles for breakfast because Australian summers are ridiculously hot.

Sometimes I hide in the bathroom with the light off just to get two minutes to myself,

And then spend date night with your daddy scrolling through photos of you on our phones because we miss you so much.

But all the time, I have to pinch myself because I can't believe I get to be your mama.

All the time I wake up with thankfulness in my heart for another day with you.

Twenty-Six: **Magnificent One**

A ballad about beauty

I knew it from the start
You were one of a kind
The magnificent kind
Forging your own path through the world
Bounding, leaping, twirling into our hearts
Leaving us in your wake
In absolute awe.

You emit your light unashamedly
Neither bushels nor breezes can extinguish it
Knowing exactly who you are with no apologies
You let it shine.

A beauty rarer than the finest of jewels
Though the world may not be ready or deserving
Though they may not even grasp it fully
Still you share it, as you should.

Spread your wings and take flight
Keep up with your bounding, leap higher, twirl and twirl and twirl again
The world needs your beauty
And someday, if they're lucky, they may understand it.

Twenty-Seven: Tears

A lyric on emotions

Mommy may cry, sweetheart.
But that's okay.
The sun always breaks through the clouds
And rain must come before the rainbow.

Mommy may cry, sweet one.
But don't you fret.
What is life if we don't feel things deeply
To live means to know both loss and joy, loneliness and beauty.

Mommy may cry, darling.
But that's alright.
To be disappointed in the way life turned out or feel like you've let yourself down
To mourn what was or long for what could have been.

Mommy may cry, my child.
Tears of joy.
Because life is full of such incredible beauty
And tears may be the only suitable response from a heart in complete awe.

Mommy may cry
Because of being unbelievably proud

Of who you are and who you're becoming

And getting to witness firsthand every step of your marvellous journey.

Mommy cries and so can you.

Let the tears fall, sweetheart, one by one.

There is no shame

Our Heavenly Father catches them all.

Because sorrow may last for the night, but His joy comes with the morning.

when she turned to face the sun, she could see she had
already been given everything it would take.

Twenty-Eight: Choosing You

A shape poem about priorities

Our days are full of choices.
Big, medium and small. Greater or lesser. Insignificant or life-altering.
Choices that weave together, one strand at a time, to form the tapestry of our
lives. At the end of the day, may our choices reflect what matters most.

Choices.
Choosing patience.
Giving love and then giving more of it.
Choosing grace rather than demanding perfection.
Choosing another cuddle instead of coveting my own space.
Delivering my words with gentleness regardless of my inner feelings.
Being generous with my time, my energy, my thoughts and not hoarding them.
Choosing to join you for another round of UNO instead of tackling that pile of dishes.
Choosing to watch you play ninjas in the backyard rather than being distracted by my phone.
Choosing to care most what my family thinks rather than being
concerned with the opinions of rest of the world.
Showing you how to do a cartwheel, albeit pulling a muscle, instead of just telling you what to do.
Choosing to listen to your concerns, as small as they may seem, knowing the size they are to you.
Acknowledging that your big feelings are often reflecting a deeper truth in your life.
Singing one more song to get you to sleep even when my voice is tired.
Choosing to be the person that I'm asking you to be.
Choosing to explain the 'why' behind my 'no'.
Giving you my undivided attention.
Choosing family.
Choices.

Twenty-Nine: **Help Me**

A prayer for sustenance

Father,

Help me to know what to say, when all known words fail me.

And to be the steady strong one that they need, when my knees are quivering.

Teach me to not just hear their words, but to listen to their hearts.

Help me to know when to speak, and when it's time to stay quiet.

Let me discern when to intervene, and when it's best to let them learn.

Give me the knowledge to know when to hold them close and the power to step back when needed.

My weaknesses taunt me day after day,

But grant me your endless patience when my supply runs dry.

The insecurities of who I'm not and what I should be plague me,

But may my children look at me and see strength that comes only from You.

No matter what may befall me,

Because of Your lovingkindness, Your compassion, Your steadfastness,

May they see firsthand the wonder of who You are.

Please give me your grace, upon grace, upon grace

For all my days unending.

Bestow it on me for the sake of these children

For they are your charge

And, for now, you've placed them in my arms.

Only by Your side can I love them as they deserve,

with the unconditional measure from Your heart.

In the name of Jesus, whose love changed everything, Amen.

Thirty: The Back of Her Head

Comparisons on now and then

Growing up, I have so many memories of being in the car. All major and minor events in my life were often sandwiched by car rides to and from. Road trips in the summer, commutes back and forth from school, Sunday mornings to church, convoys to school graduations, and transport to those never-ending birthday parties. I remember that pure, sometimes nearly uncontainable feeling of anticipation on the way to these places to the point where I would be unbuckling my seatbelt simultaneously with the turn of the key to shut off the engine.

There's nothing catastrophic or seemingly that significant about these memories, but what I also recall from these trips is watching my mom. Maybe it was simply because I was constrained by my seat belt and the view of her head was perpetually locked in front of me. Or maybe it was because those car rides held more meaning than I could comprehend at the time. Sitting behind her I'd watch her side profile as she looked out the window when my dad was driving. She was usually quiet with a smile playing softly on her lips. Sunlight would shine through silhouetting her face and I remember being in a continual state of absolute awe of her. To me, she was the definition of beauty, she was everything I hoped and aspired to become, she was the one who held it all together for me.

Now, as a mother myself, my experience in the car is far different from that when I was a kid. While all I saw then was the back of her head, I now understand just how much must have been going through her heart and her mind. Because today, in our comings and goings, as I drive or ride, there are often countless thoughts running through *my* head. Looking out the window, here is where I have a few moments to consider if my ducks are in a row or if all my ducks are even accounted for. In this time, I contemplate the state of the hearts of each of my kids while simultaneously dreading the state of the house I'll be coming home to after a whirlwind morning exodus out the door. This is where I find myself internally defending the lack of credibility of the speeding ticket that came in the mail last week and hoping I remembered to dress the kids in the right school uniforms. In the car I plan our meals for the week ahead and brainstorm what birthday presents I need to buy on the weekend. Sometimes being in the car is the only time in my day where I can physically stop and consciously breathe.

I didn't know back then what I know now. I didn't know that being a mom would be so much. And I can say, without a doubt, that I'm even more in awe of my mom now than I was then. I had no idea how much there would be to know, to consider, to organise and to take stock of, but I know now. I didn't realise the weight she carried and the extent of the responsibility that fell on her shoulders every day, but I feel it now. I didn't understand so much of what had to happen behind the scenes to make my car rides filled with such excitement and expectation, but I get it now.

Undoubtedly my kids see the back of my head in our car rides these days too. While they often take that time to advise me if my hair is out of place or a tag is sticking out, I hope that one day they will look back and realise how it was all for them. All the planning, the working, the hustling all the car rides- it was all to give them the very best life we could. I hope one day they too will look back and understand the amount of space they occupy in our hearts.

Part 3:

Maturation

Glorious flowers in full bloom producing seeds and ripening; ready to give back to the world.

Thirty-One: **Taller and Wiser**

An end-of-the-school-year reflection

"Stay little forever." I always say to you.

"We can't mum."

"I know."

It's somehow the end of another school year.

You've grown taller, your feet are at least two sizes bigger, and
your cheeks are, regretfully, a little less squishy.

You remind me that you're smarter now too and I remind you that you're even cheekier than before.

You've learned all about underwater ecosystems, know your rainbow addition
facts and use clever words like 'fabulous' and 'chaos' in a sentence.

You've mastered important skills like landing a forward flip and the art of convincing
your dad to buy you banana bread before school in the mornings.

You've learned that kids can be mean and other hard lessons, but I see your heart getting stronger for it.

You carry your bags by yourself and don't need me to hold your hand as much but I'm always going to try.

These years keep passing by and I'll still be here. Collecting your ever-changing
school photos and with them the priceless memories each one holds.

But if you want to stay little forever, I really won't mind.

Thirty-Two: Longer

A response to the brevity of time

Just a little bit longer.
Will you stay in my arms?
Will you hold onto my hand
Will you stay by my side?

For the sun rises and then sets
Again and again.
Days turn to nights,
weeks roll into months
then carry into years that never seem to stop.

Just a little longer,
Will you need me there?
To guide and comfort you, to reassure and support you
Will you want me to be with you?

My arms expand as you grow
And grow and grow.
Then you won't need my hand
And you'll be too big for my arms.

So just a little bit longer
Will you stay?
Will you hold onto my hand
Will you stay by my side?

Together they followed every last ray of the sunlight because they knew that summer wouldn't last forever.

Thirty-Three: **Suddenly**

Thoughts on the passing of time

It happened all the sudden and yet little by little at the same time.

I hadn't even noticed though perhaps I hadn't wanted to.

Until one day you're standing in front of me,

Saying you can walk to the frozen section of the shop by yourself to collect the blueberries,

And that you can 'most definitely' ride your bike around the block without me.

You can do your own hair now and can pick the perfect accessories to match your outfits.

You don't need me to hold your hand as you ascend the escalator stairs, the same ones that used to make you shrink back with fear.

You're writing your name all by yourself with a pencil grip that doesn't need the support of my hand.

And you know how to use just the right words and puppy face to persuade me to buy you that special little something.

I look in the mirror and I've changed too.

Some days it feels sudden, but I know it's happened gradually over time.

The grey hairs have lost their subtlety and shamelessly pop through my once purely chocolate hair.

The wrinkles firmly nestled in the corners of my eyes expose themselves each time I smile.

The movements of life feel more effortful, and my body doesn't bounce back with the same elasticity that it used to.

Though time has escaped me, I recognise all these traits as hallmarks of a beautiful story,

The mementos of tales from my early days of motherhood,

Reverberating echoes from the very sweetest of days.

With gratitude for the night and expectant wonder
for the day she welcomes the morning.

Thirty-Four: **Dear Mamas**

Words of gratitude

To the women I have journeyed with in this season of motherhood:

If only I could give you all the flowers in the world. There are so many words to be said and so many words that will remain unspoken, but I pray can somehow still be heard.

Having a village around me in the early years of motherhood has meant more to me than I ever expected. To those I've walked with for a brief season or those who are still alongside me today; to those I've literally stood side by side with or those I've connected with across greater distances, I am eternally indebted to you. Please accept my words as an offering of gratitude and a celebration of all that we have shared.

Thank you, mamas,

For showing up time after time,

And for hearing and listening and not casting judgment.

Thank you for letting me into your world just as I've opened up mine,

For loving my children as if they were your own and entrusting me to love yours.

Thank you for not turning away even after being confronted by my weaknesses,

For your gentleness when I tried to prove I had it all together,

And for your graciousness when my children smeared food on your carpet and turned your playroom upside down.

Thank you for giving up your time and energy to care for me and my babies,

For lending spare clothes, sharing snacks and offering wet wipes,

And for leading the way with your example of steadfastness and faithfulness as you inspired me to be better.

Thank you for taking time to share and empathise with me,

And for giving permission for us to laugh at each other about trivial day to day faux-pas or cry together over heartbreaks of every size.

Thank you for teaching me the freedom of not actually caring what my house looks like when people come over,

But to care most about the important things like drying tears, giving extra cuddles and leaning in closer to listen.

Thank you, for speaking words of life when I have struggled to see daylight,

And for giving of yourselves when I have been unable to give equally in return.

Thank you for sticking with me through all of my moments,

And for opening your homes and your hearts to let me share with you in all of yours.

Thank you for telling me the truth when I've needed to hear it,

And at the same time for not taking me too seriously.

Thank you for the genuineness you've shown in a world that's too often filled with falsities and insincerity,

And for demonstrating with your life the beauty of a mother who pursues things of eternal value.

Thank you for each laugh, each tear, each story we've shared

And as we turn the page and venture into chapters that are just beginning to be written, may we continue to champion and honour each other in all that's ahead.

Thirty-Five: **What It's Like**

Things no one told you (but maybe they did)

No one tells you what it's like
To love someone so much
That your heart will be so tightly bound to another person's wellbeing
That you will feel deeply every hurt that pierces through their heart as if it's your own
And that you'll have to live reconciled with the knowledge that you would give your very life for them.

No one tells you what it's like
When you have to balance it all
That the demands will often be greater than the supply
That you'll have to let go of some things to make room for others
And it will be constant give and take, adapting and improvising.

No one tells you what it's like
That life is truly no longer about you
That you will have to give of yourself when you feel there's nothing left to give
And that you will learn the meaning of sacrifice in deep places
But you will come out the other side even when it all seems impossible to do.

No one tells you what it's like
How the wonder outweighs it all
That the hardest of days can't undo the beauty
The daily grind, the constant chaos, the ups and downs, it's worth it all
And that the greatest thing you'll ever do is to love the little ones you've created.

From a distance she was one among thousands,
but to them she was the only one.

Thirty-Six: **Seabound**

A metaphor about letting go

I release your hand
But you're just off the shore
Still within my reach
Only three steps away from me
When you're there I know what to do.

The time comes and I take a few steps back
I watch you closely
Your dancing shadow is now your closest companion
Your steps slide through glistening ripples as you twirl and leap on your own
Water droplets splashing up in translucent bouquets surround you.

You move beyond my reach
I keep my toes anchored in the sand
The sea wraps around you as you drift farther out
Your smile is cathartic as your float on your back
The water gleefully tracing your outline, waves swaying you as if in a waltz.

If I'm honest I know this is always how it was meant to be
You holding my hand on the dry sand was never the forever plan
I've seen the longing in your eyes as you've looked to where the ocean collides gloriously with the horizon
Contemplating the endless possibilities that await you out there
I've known you were made for more than the sand could offer.

And at some point

You'll come back from your explorations in deeper water

We'll collect shells together again

You'll show me what you've studied and ecosystems you've unearthed

Once again you'll be within my reach.

I'll always stand convinced

that the greatest marvel of all isn't the vastness of the sea

or the brilliance of the skies

but the one whose eyes are reflecting the ocean,

Whose heart was made to explore its boundless depths.

And in all your comings and goings

I will stay on the shore

Though you're no longer in my reach

And I'll watch you dive deeper and swim farther

I'll miss being covered in sand and the saltiness of my hair after our days together in the sun though I never thought I would

And I'll wait for your returns.

Thirty-Seven: **I'll Be the One**

A mama's vow

When you try your very best, but it all goes unnoticed,
I will see you.

When you feel like your voice is drowned out by all the others and you have nothing worthy to say,
I will hear you.

When you have had all the best intentions but are still misunderstood,
I will know you.

When the pain is too much for your heart to bear,
I will hold you.

When life is confusing and lonely and you don't know what road you should choose,
I will walk beside you.

When you think you don't measure up or have what it takes,
I will believe in you.

When no one wants you to be on their team and your friends have turned away,
I will claim you.

When you haven't succeeded or you've made a mistake, when life is hard or you've been let down.
I will love you.
I will *always* be the one to love you.

Thirty-Eight: **With You**

A song of inspiration

Through your eyes I can see the world in a different light, one that's new and promising and filled with every possibility.

Holding your hand, I'm grounded in the everyday goodness of moments that come and go in an instant, and reminded to centre my life on the only things that matter in the end.

In your voice I hear curiosity and wonder that revives my soul, giving me hope and expectation for the future of our world.

Through your words I hear wisdom that is simple and pure and brings perspective in much needed places.

From your mind I am amazed at the endless flow of ideas that usher in the promise of original things to be built, discovered and changed through your life.

Through your heart I'm convicted, humbled and sharpened, to be a better person, to love without limits and to see the best in everyone I meet.

With you in my life, I am forever changed.

It was her life's greatest joy, to give it all away.

Thirty-Nine: My Best Days

Thoughts on unexpected wonder

Who knew that the best days of my life would happen most unexpectantly.

When perhaps I looked my worst,

After eternally sleepless nights, holding you close for hours until you finally drifted off.

Or after painstakingly waiting in line for ages for that ride but then squealing
at the top of our lungs with glee through the whole thing.

That my best days would entail being covered in every kind of messy substance known to mankind
but knowing the fingerprints and smudges on my shoulder were the result of being needed.

That my best moments would be spent keeping watch for little creatures every evening before bathtime
through the big window on our staircase and hearing your cries of glee each time you spotted one.

Or that the best thing would simply be curling up on the couch together with your favourite
book that we would read over and over again until we both had it memorised.

Who knew that I'd spend my best days walking our streets in search of Christmas lights getting
caught up in the wonder radiating from your face under black skies blanketed with stars.

And that my best moments would be us stretched out on the carpet sorting
LEGO together for hours as I listened to all your stories.

I would never have guessed that my best days would be spent wildly chasing crabs back into
their holes and holding hands, as we let our feet get stuck in the water-covered sand.

Or standing side by side and watching bats fly overhead in purple-coloured
skies as the sun peeks its final glance above the horizon

Who knew that of all the things I dreamed of becoming when I grew up,

spending my days as your mama would by far be my best.

Forty: Of All the Things I Could Say

A handover of wisdom learned

I walked into the shop to grab a few things before heading down to the beach on my day off. All three kids had been dropped off successfully at school and surprisingly the morning traffic hadn't even been that bad. I walked quickly down the aisles wanting to get to the waves before the equatorial heat consumed the day. My attention shifted quickly hearing a clamour behind me. I turned around and saw her there, bent over, cradling a baby who was nestled in a carrier on her front. Another little one was swinging her legs exuberantly from her perch in the shopping trolley and a third child stood next to her crying with tins of soup piled around her feet, obviously the source of the clamour.

I rushed over to help her clean up the mess and hesitated briefly with the familiarity of it all. She looked at me with a mixture of relief and guilt in her eyes. I told her I had been there many times. Just as quickly as it had happened, everything was back in order, and I picked up the sippy cup that had fallen from the trolley. Just as I was handing it to her, I remembered.

My heart was full of so many things I wanted to tell her, so many things I wanted her to know and re-assure her of, but with a full heart, I looked up at her and whispered, 'These *are* the best days of your life.'

She looked at me taken aback but smiled politely. I turned and headed towards the front of the shop.

One day she will know too.

Forty-One: **Sunflower Days**

Finale

Sunflower days

Starting so small, tiny seeds in the ground

Bursting forth into eager green shoots

Growing and changing with each passing day

Radiant blooms

Reaching, stretching, bending

Glistening with golds and endless shades of yellow

Illuminated against a bright blue sky

Chasing the sun

Blowing with the wind

Sunflower days

Forever imprinted on my heart.

Alicia Easton is a primary teacher and paediatric speech pathologist originally from the United States who now resides in sunny Australia. Devoted wife to her husband Michael and mother of three young children, she uses her faith and motherhood experiences to connect with others through heartfelt writing.

Printed in the United States
by Baker & Taylor Publisher Services